You're Hopeless, Charlie Brown!

Charles M. Schulz

Selected cartoons from YOU'RE WEIRD, SIR!
Volume 3

CORONET BOOKS
Hodder and Stoughton

PEANUTS Comic Strips by Charles M. Schulz

Copyright © 1981, 1982 by United Feature
Syndicate, Inc.

First published in the United States of
America by Ballantine Books 1984.
Coronet edition 1985

British Library C.I.P.

Schulz, Charles M.
  [You're weird, Sir! *Selections*] You're
  hopeless, Charlie Brown! : selected cartoons
  from you're weird, sir! volume 3.
  I. [You're weird, Sir. *Selections*] II. Title
  741.5'973   PN6728.P4

ISBN 0-340-37887-5

You're Hopeless, CHARLIE BROWN!

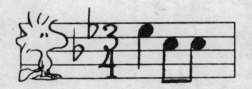

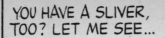

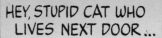

YOU'RE SUPPOSED TO MEET YOUR COUSIN AT THE STATION?

BUT YOU DON'T KNOW WHAT SHE LOOKS LIKE, AND SHE DOESN'T KNOW WHAT YOU LOOK LIKE...

TELL HER SHE'LL RECOGNIZE YOU BECAUSE YOU'LL BE HOLDING A COPY OF "WAR AND PEACE"

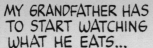

MY GRANDFATHER HAS TO START WATCHING WHAT HE EATS...

THE DOCTOR TOLD HIM HE SHOULD CHANGE HIS LIFE-STYLE

MY GRANDFATHER HATES TO TAKE ADVICE

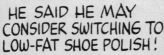

HE SAID HE MAY CONSIDER SWITCHING TO LOW-FAT SHOE POLISH!

BAM BAM
BAM BAM

IS IT SUPPERTIME ALREADY?

OKAY! OKAY! YOU DON'T HAVE TO BREAK DOWN THE DOOR!

I'VE NEVER SEEN ANYONE SO IMPATIENT

HERE

I READ THE FIRST TWO CHAPTERS OF YOUR NEW NOVEL..THEY WERE TERRIBLE!

NOVELS SHOULD BE FUNNY, SAD, WITTY AND EXPRESSIVE

"SICK" DOESN'T COUNT?

YOU SHOULD GO OVER AND TALK WITH THAT LITTLE RED-HAIRED GIRL, CHARLIE BROWN

ASK HER TO EAT LUNCH WITH YOU

TELL HER YOU'D BE HAPPY JUST TO BE WITH HER FOR AN HOUR OR SO

AN HOUR? I'D SETTLE FOR AN "OR SO"!

WHICH WOULD YOU RATHER HAVE, A STOMACHACHE OR A HEADACHE?

I DON'T KNOW...A HEADACHE, I GUESS

GOOD! I'LL PUT YOU DOWN FOR A HEADACHE

IT'S NICE HAVING SOMEONE IN CHARGE WHO'S SO CONSIDERATE

"PIGPEN"! I HAVEN'T SEEN YOU FOR A LONG TIME...

OBVIOUSLY, YOU ARE JUST AS MESSY AS EVER!

THE WORLD NEEDS MESSY PEOPLE...

OTHERWISE THE NEAT PEOPLE WOULD TAKE OVER!

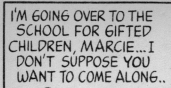

SHE WENT OVER TO A SCHOOL FOR GIFTED CHILDREN, CHARLES..SHE THINKS THEY'RE GOING TO GIVE HER THINGS...

I DON'T KNOW WHAT TO DO ABOUT HER, CHARLES.. SHE NEVER LISTENS...

CHARLES? ARE YOU THERE? WHO AM I TALKING TO?

IF I BARK, IT'LL SCARE HER TO DEATH...

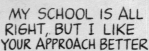

YES, MA'AM, I READ IN THE PAPER ABOUT YOUR SCHOOL FOR GIFTED CHILDREN

MY SCHOOL IS ALL RIGHT, BUT I LIKE YOUR APPROACH BETTER

IS THIS BAG GOING TO BE BIG ENOUGH FOR ALL THE GIFTS?

THESE ARE MY CLOTHING AND SHOE SIZES..IF YOU GIVE OUT ICE SKATES, I'D LIKE THEM ABOUT ONE SIZE SMALLER...

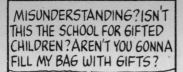

MARCIE, YOU LET ME GO TO THAT SCHOOL, AND MAKE A FOOL OF MYSELF!

YOU WOULDN'T LISTEN TO ME, SIR

YOU DIDN'T TRY HARD ENOUGH

YOU COULD HAVE STOPPED ME IF YOU HAD REALLY TRIED

IF I HAD TRIED TO STOP YOU, YOU WOULD HAVE HIT ME...

YOU COULD HAVE DUCKED

SHE'S GONE, CHARLES! PEPPERMINT PATTY HAS LEFT TOWN!

BUT I JUST TALKED TO HER YESTERDAY...

I THINK SHE WAS MORE DEPRESSED THAN WE THOUGHT, CHARLES... WHERE DO YOU THINK SHE WENT?

"SPIKE'S REAL ESTATE..NEEDLES, CALIFORNIA"...WELL, I'M NOT REALLY READY TO BUY... COULDN'T YOU JUST FIND ME A PLACE TO STAY?

CHARLIE BROWN, HAS ANYONE EVER TOLD YOU THAT YOU WALK FUNNY?

YOU DON'T HAVE ANY RHYTHM! YOUR FEET POINT IN ALL THE WRONG DIRECTIONS..YOUR ARMS SWING THE WRONG WAY...

STAND UP STRAIGHT..NOW MOVE FORWARD...WALK THE WAY I TOLD YOU...

IN SOUTHWEST CAMEROON THERE ARE FROGS THAT WEIGH TEN POUNDS

THAT IS DEFINITELY NOT SOMETHING TO BE TOLD JUST BEFORE YOU GO TO SLEEP

SCHULZ

I HAVE IT ALL FIGURED OUT, MARCIE...

THE WAY I SEE IT, THERE SEEM TO BE MORE QUESTIONS THAN THERE ARE ANSWERS

SO?

SO TRY TO BE THE ONE WHO ASKS THE QUESTIONS!

WHAT SHOULD I WRITE?

WRITE WHAT YOU FEEL

Dear Little Red-Haired Girl,
I love you very much.

NOW, ALL YOU HAVE TO DO IS SLIP THE NOTE INTO THE MAIL SLOT IN THE FRONT DOOR OF HER HOUSE...

HERE WE GO FOR THE FIRST HOCKEY GAME OF THE SEASON...

I CAN SEE MYSELF NOW OUT ON THE OL' POND RACING DOWN THE ICE WITH THE PUCK!

AFTER IT GETS A LITTLE COLDER

ARE YOU AWARE THAT HALLOWEEN IS COMING?

ON HALLOWEEN THE "GREAT PUMPKIN" RISES OUT OF THE PUMPKIN PATCH, AND BRINGS TOYS TO ALL THE CHILDREN IN THE WORLD!

I FIND THAT HARD TO BELIEVE

MY SWEET BABBOO SAYS IT'S TRUE

HOWEVER, I'M NOT YOUR SWEET BABBOO!

MY SWEET BABBOO SAYS IF WE SIT HERE IN THE PUMPKIN PATCH, WE MAY SEE THE "GREAT PUMPKIN"

I DON'T KNOW..

YOU CAN PROBABLY SEE A LOT OF STRANGE THINGS IN A PUMPKIN PATCH...

BONSOIR, MADEMOISELLE... IS THIS, BY CHANCE, THE ROAD TO PARIS?

THIS IS RIDICULOUS! I'VE WASTED ALL THIS TIME SITTING HERE IN A PUMPKIN PATCH!

I TOLD YOU THERE'S NO "GREAT PUMPKIN"!

WHAT AM I GOING TO DO THE REST OF THE EVENING?

"AIMERIEZ-VOUS ALLER DANSER?" WOULD YOU LIKE TO GO DANCING?

OKAY, MARCIE, WE'RE GONNA PRACTICE THE OL' 'STATUE OF LIBERTY' PLAY...

YOU FADE BACK TO PASS, AND I COME RUNNING AROUND AND GRAB THE BALL

MARCIE! YOU'RE SUPPOSED TO LET GO OF THE BALL!

Gentlemen,
Regarding the
recent rejection
slip you sent me.

I think there
might have been a
misunderstanding.

What I really
wanted was for you
to publish my story,
and send me fifty
thousand dollars.

Didn't you
realize that?

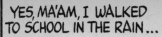

WHAT ELSE SHOWS MORE DEVOTION?

TO GET UP IN THE MIDDLE OF THE NIGHT, AND TAKE A BLANKET OUT TO A FREEZING FRIEND...

NOTHING, UNLESS, IN YOUR SLEEPY CONDITION, YOU PLACE IT ON THE WRONG END!

SCHULZ

YES, MA'AM, I'VE BEEN READING THE BOOK...

WELL, NOT ACTUALLY THE BOOK YET...

I READ THE ACKNOWLEDGMENTS, THE TRANSLATOR'S NOTES, THE INTRODUCTION, THE PREFACE, THE FOREWORD AND THE DEDICATION...

IT'S BEEN UPHILL ALL THE WAY!

HERE ARE THE WORLD FAMOUS HOCKEY PLAYERS SKATING OUT FOR THE BIG GAME...

THEY STAND AT CENTER ICE FOR THE NATIONAL ANTHEM

WOODSTOCK ALWAYS PRETENDS HE KNOWS THE WORDS...

YOU'RE A BIRD, AND THAT'S A BIRD'S JOB...

YOU'RE SUPPOSED TO SING BRIGHT CHEERFUL SONGS EVERY MORNING TO HELP PEOPLE START THEIR DAY...

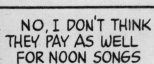

NO, I DON'T THINK THEY PAY AS WELL FOR NOON SONGS

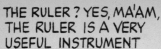

I THINK YOUR FALLING ASLEEP IN CLASS IS A REAL PROBLEM, SIR

DON'T WORRY ABOUT IT, MARCIE

BUT I DO..

ONE WOULD ALMOST GET THE IMPRESSION THAT YOU COME TO SCHOOL PREPARED TO SLEEP...

WHAT MAKES YOU SAY THAT, MARCIE?

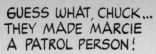

GUESS WHAT, CHUCK...
THEY MADE MARCIE
A PATROL PERSON!

CAN YOU IMAGINE
THAT? CAN YOU REALLY
IMAGINE THAT, CHUCK?

WELL, I DON'T KNOW...
SHE'S A VERY GOOD
STUDENT..I SUPPOSE
SHE DESERVES IT...

I HATE TALKING
TO YOU, CHUCK!

MARCIE, I DON'T NEED YOU TO HELP ME ACROSS THE STREET!

RULES ARE RULES! I'M THE PATROL PERSON, AND I'LL TELL YOU WHEN YOU CAN GO ACROSS!

ALL RIGHT, EVERYBODY, LET'S GO! QUICKLY NOW! TO THE OTHER SIDE! QUICKLY NOW! QUICKLY!

IT'S ONLY THREE O'CLOCK, BUT AS SOON AS I GET HOME, I'M GOING TO BED!

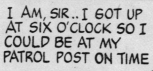

PSST, MARCIE! THE TEACHER JUST CALLED YOUR NAME!

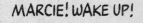

MARCIE! WAKE UP!

SORRY, MA'AM..

RIGHT NOW, I'D SAY SHE'S THE MAYOR OF "ZONK CITY"!

SCHULZ

OKAY, TROOPS, LET'S GO! MOVE ACROSS! LET'S GO! LET'S GO!

YOU SEEM TO BE DOING A GOOD JOB AS MY SUBSTITUTE, SIR...

THANK YOU, MARCIE.. IT RUNS IN THE FAMILY... MY GRAMPA WAS AN MP IN WORLD WAR II.

THAT DOESN'T MEAN, SIR, THAT YOU HAVE TO CHECK FOR IDENTIFICATION PAPERS...

IT'S JUST TOO BAD THAT I'M ONLY A SUBSTITUTE PATROL PERSON, CHUCK..IT REALLY IS!

I'D STRAIGHTEN THINGS OUT IN A HURRY!

YOUR GRAMPA WAS AN MP IN WORLD WAR II, WASN'T HE?

THAT'S RIGHT, CHUCK, AND NO GI EVER GOT INTO THE PX BEFORE NOON WHEN **HE** WAS ON DUTY!

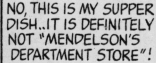

"SANTA BUG" IS COMING TO MENDELSON'S DEPARTMENT STORE?

THAT'S VERY EXCITING, LITTLE BUG, BUT YOU'RE NOT IN MENDELSON'S DEPARTMENT STORE...

YOU'RE IN MY SUPPER DISH!

NO, I DON'T KNOW WHERE THE DESIGNER JEANS DEPARTMENT IS...

LOOK, STUPID LITTLE BUG, IF YOU'RE WAITING FOR "SANTA BUG" TO APPEAR IN MY SUPPER DISH, YOU'VE GOT A LONG WAIT!

HE IS? WHERE?

HO HO HO HO HO

IT'S AWFULLY TEMPTING TO ASK HIM FOR AN ELECTRIC TRAIN...

SCHULZ

Dear Grandma,
Thank you for the stationery and the pen and pencil set.

Now I can write lots of letters.

I HATE WRITING LETTERS!

Thank you again. Happy New Year. love, Sally

MAJOR FUNDING FOR THIS MEAL WAS PROVIDED BY A GRANT FROM OUR FAMILY

IF THEY HAVE A PLEDGE NIGHT, I'M LEAVING!